T0067949

The Integration of Christian & Secular Education

Leadership in the 21st Century

Patrick T. Brown, MDiv, Ed.D

WESTBOW
PRESS®
A DIVISION OF THOMAS NELSON
& ZONDERVAN

Scripture quotations taken from the New American Standard Bible® (NASB), Copyright © 1960, 1962, 1963, 1968, 1971, 1972, 1973, 1975, 1977, 1995 by The Lockman Foundation Used by permission. www.Lockman.org

WestBow Press books may be ordered through booksellers or by contacting:

WestBow Press
A Division of Thomas Nelson & Zondervan
1663 Liberty Drive
Bloomington, IN 47403
www.westbowpress.com
1 (866) 928-1240

ISBN: 978-1-9736-2312-0 (sc)
ISBN: 978-1-9736-2311-3 (e)

Print information available on the last page.

WestBow Press rev. date: 03/27/2018

Dedication

This book is dedicated to my family and church family, for your undiminishing support.

Introduction

I'm compelled to continue, both Christian and secular education are my passion, so it sometimes moves me when I hear others who disrespect and disregard the whole concept or speak flippantly about it.

Christian schools are recognized by some to be inferior or unnecessary. To some, they're considered too expensive, too strict, too intrusive, or too contradicting.

While no school is perfect, Christian Education plays a vital role in the training of our youth and I believe it is absolutely essential for our growth and development.

This is not to ignore or disrespect those who choose or desire, to work in the public schools. But when it comes to the future of our youth today, we must make Christian education paramount.

The devil himself is the chief deceiver, and he desperately wants us to think that Christian education is not important and that the public schools can educate our children just fine without Christian teachers and leaders. He will use every technique and argument he can to deceive us into complacency.

But we cannot afford to waiver concerning education.

Christian education is vitally important because:

The public school system has an agenda – and it's not just about education nor evolution.

I've heard parents say that they know their children are hearing about evolution in the public school, but they discuss these issues at home, so everything is just fine.

If this were correct everything would be fine, but it's just not.

Yes, our youth are good at refuting evolution and staying true to their beliefs in The Creator, but that's not the problem.

The issue is that the public school system is pushing more than evolution, and most parents don't even know the assault of dangerous philosophies that their young people are facing.

The public-school system is humanistic at its core and pushes its progressive agenda every way it possibly can. From a very early age, students are taught that there is no absolute truth, whether physically or spiritually, that homosexuality is an acceptable alternative lifestyle, that some people are more valuable than others, and that socialism is the key to the future of our society.

And the problem is that these philosophies are taught very subtly and weaved into illustrations and application questions.

A mature adult may or may not even be aware of them, much less a child.

This subtle teaching of humanism, socialism, and progressivism is dangerously persuasive to impressionable children, adolescents and teens.

Since we as parents are not in the classroom with students, we don't know what to refute.

Our youth need to do more than just survive. Can our youth today survive the ever-rising onslaught of unbiblical philosophies and graduate from a public school with their faith intact? Of course.

But don't we expect more than this? Yes

Since when is the goal to raise kids who barely "made it"? Don't we want kids who understand God's truths and how to apply them to every situation in life?

Don't we want our kids to have a deep, meaningful relationship with God?

Don't we want them to be everything they can be and to use their lives for His glory? Yes

I'm not saying a kid who attends a public school cannot be used by God. That would be ridiculous.

But what I am conveying is that the main purpose of Christian schools should be to intentionally disciple students. Effective Christian schools should be using every opportunity to speak Biblical truth into students' lives and help them to become more like Christ.

Christian schools should not just be the absence of wrong

philosophies. They should instead be the infusion of truth into every aspect of the day from academics to peer relationships to sports. A student who learns to hear and apply Biblical truths has done a lot more than survive. He or she must be ready to thrive.

In my best attempt, Research has revealed that Christian education and leadership is declining as a life ordering force among the Christian community, (Barra Group, 2009; Ham & Beemer, 2009; Smithwick, 2008). This trend continues despite the ubiquitous references to terms like Biblical integration and biblical worldviews in Christian schools' mission statements. In fact, from its inception, the Christian school movement has emphasized the importance of Biblical integration as a means of developing a biblical worldview as a major motive for Christian education and leadership.

If developing a biblical worldview is of such great importance to the body of Christ and if teaching and learning from biblical principles provides a pathway to attain this goal, then it is imperative that the principles used for biblical integration are biblically valid.

The purpose of this study is to address the need for Christian education and leadership, to validate biblical principles used in Christian schools and to consider community curriculum development in Christian schools.

This study is an expedition of the influence and affluence of Christian education in the 21st century toward leadership development.

A small, purposive example of 10 individuals who are in some position of educational leadership and who received a Christian, elementary and secondary education were interviewed about their perceptions of the integration of Christian education in the 21st century toward leadership development.

The responses of the participants revealed relevant themes to the centrality of this study: integration of Christian worldview, influence of teachers, academic experience, and activities in the educational process.

Keywords

Leadership, education, Christian education, relationship, biblical integration

Introduction to the Research

The 21st century demands a higher level of leadership preparation.

We live in a global, interconnected world that is increasingly urban and diverse. Colleges and universities are no longer confined to cities, regions or states; virtual universities abound. Today's college students learn best when their professors work side-by-side with them and engage them in learning through research, internships, study abroad, service learning, team projects, and learning communities. While lecturing is still important in the classroom, experiential learning, team projects and high-tech information gathering are critical elements of learning for today's students.

Taking advantage of online delivery and alternative class-time structures will become more important as well.

University graduates are unlikely to retain the same job or even the same career for more than a few years.

For that reason, graduates must learn how to become critical thinkers who understand how to handle rapid change in their lives and their professional fields of study.

The broad culture is predominantly postmodern culture in which rationality and truth can be seen as problematic.

The world is becoming post-Christian, as well. The center of Christianity has shifted from the United States to Africa and South America. Because of the post-Christian direction in which our culture is moving and the secularization of so many formerly Christian universities, it is especially important that God's people remain Christ-centered.

Despite the challenges facing Christian higher education in the next decade, with homosexuality and same sex marriage, we must engage the minds and hearts of students in such a way that they will become Christian leaders.

Students must be prepared to address the inevitable secularization occurring across the globe.

They must be prepared as missional leaders who will live out their Christian beliefs in a world fraught with scandals, corporate ethical failures, and challenging moral dilemmas.

First, for Christian education to thrive in the 21st century, extreme emphasis must be placed on understanding the foundations on which Christian education was established.

A renewed mission and vision must be communicated to all including the school board, administrators, parents, students, and teachers.

To formulate a more complete Christian education philosophy for the modern era, current Christian education professionals were interviewed.

Questions

How has being a Christian affected your work environment, if any?

Do you feel particularly called to Christian education? Why?

What is your understanding of the philosophical differences between Christian and secular education?

What are the main characteristics that distinguish a Christian school from a public school?

Who has most influenced you to become an educator, and how did they influence you?

How would you describe a person who has a "teachable spirit"?

How close do you think you come to that description? How do you respond to constructive criticism?

What types of "people situations" frustrate or sadden you the most and how do you handle them Biblically?

What would your previous employer or college advisor say were your greatest strengths for teaching, and what areas would they suggest were areas that need growth? And do you agree with those assessments?

What is your approach to classroom management and student discipline?

Tell me about a difficult circumstance you handled. What action did you take? What were the results?

Describe for me a lesson you taught that went very well. Why did the lesson work so well?

What methods of teaching, besides lecture, would you use to present material to your students?

What if your students don't "get it"? In other words, if a lesson is not working for all your students, do you have a plan for remediation? How do you carry out that plan?

Why has the relationship between law enforcement and citizens come under such scrutiny?

What procedures, tactics, and techniques might be modified—or new approaches implemented—to reduce the number of instances of potentially problematic police brutality?

Can you name a person who has had a tremendous impact on you as a leader?

Maybe someone who has been a mentor to you? Why and how did this person impact your life?

What are the most important decisions you make as a leader of your organization?

As an organization gets larger there can be a tendency for the "institution" to dampen the "inspiration." How do you keep this from happening?

How do you encourage creative thinking within your organization?

Where do the great ideas come from in your organization?

Which is most important to your organization—mission, core values or vision?

How do you or other leaders in your organization communicate the "core values"?

How do you encourage others in your organization to communicate the "core values"?

Do you set aside specific times to cast vision to your employees and other leaders?

How do you ensure your organization and its activities are aligned with your "core values" How do you help a new employee understand the culture of your organization?

When faced with two equally-qualified candidates, how do you determine whom to hire?

What is one characteristic that you believe every leader should possess?

What is the biggest challenge facing leaders today?

What is one mistake you witness leaders making more frequently than others?

What is the one behavior or trait that you have seen derail more leaders' careers?

What are a few resources you would recommend to someone looking to gain insight into becoming a better leader?

What advice would you give someone going into a leadership position for the first time?

What are you doing to ensure you continue to grow and develop as a leader?

Many past visionaries, including Dr. Cordelia Moffett, Robert Bradley, Patricia Alexander, Annie Lindsey, Dr. Grey Edwards, Elizabeth Morris, Dr. Charles Kelly, Pastor Terrance Brown, Sheriff Heath Taylor and Pastor Xavier Maddox were considered through interviews having experience earlier in promoting a vision for Christian education.

Together with research and the responses of the 10 interviews for this project, a great amount of evidence exists that the transformational vision for intergration of both secular and Christian education in the 21st century is alive. We must continue to be renewed so that it may continue for generations to come. It should continue to be the place of the Christian school parent, teacher, and administrator to promote a form of schooling that focuses on the revealed truth of God in Christ.

The Academic Experience

The participants viewed their "academic experience" as an important piece of their leadership development. This was also indicated as a theme.

Although specific subjects or teachers were mentioned, there was not an emphasis on the value of the knowledge component of specific subjects; rather, the emphasis was on the importance of a strong academic program in general. There was also recognition of life applicable lessons that were learned from specific teachers or in specific subjects. Within the academic experience, the subject area was discussed more frequently and with passion. References were made toward the importance of Bible knowledge gained, life lessons of Bible application learned, and experiences within the Bible classes themselves. Some of these references included the recognition of the integration of the Bible within and throughout other academic subjects.

The participants believe that a challenging academic experience was important for developing critical thinking skills that are important to Christian leadership.

Several also suggested that they learned lessons about leadership from the academic content of courses, particularly through the examples of historical or biblical leaders.

However, they placed the highest leadership development value on their Christian experience.

We all have stories of our childhood and life experiences, and when we reflect on those experiences we make personal judgments about how those experiences mold us. For the majority of us, education is a normal and expected part of our environmental makeup and is one of the influences in our past that has had an effect on who we are as a people today.

Those involved in Christian education assume, or at least hope, they are having a transforming and shaping influence on those with whom they work, teach, preach and lead. Teachers, administrators, and parents believe Christian education has made and should make a difference in people's lives. Although this belief is widely held, there is still a question about the way in which Christian education makes a difference. The intended desire is that students, via secular or Christian Education, would be influenced in numerous ways, in their leadership development through their Christian education experience.

But how does Christian education really bring about change in people, how has it influence their direction, and how does it influence their leadership? Numerous studies have been completed on the influence of religious or faith based experiences on moral development. Researchers have looked at connections between educational experience, ethical formation, and/or critical thinking.

Studies have shown the influence of life experiences on leadership development the influence of life experiences on the development of school leadership (Williams, 1996), and the influence of educational experiences on leadership development (Bloomer, 1999. But while there has been an exponential growth in Christian schools since the 1960s (Gangel & Hendricks, 1988). The Christian church has largely accepted the Christian education movement without question, and little study seems to have been done on the influence of Christian education. (kindergarten-12th grade) education, the influence of Christian education on leadership.

This study explored the connection between Christian education and leadership development. It is generally assumed that Christian schools are an environment that intentionally works to bring coherence to a student's moral and ethical development, which is a critical component of leadership development.

Therefore, it is important to understand how the influence of that educational experience has carried over into the later development of leadership. The purpose of this study, then, was to explore the influence of Christian education on leadership development as perceived by people in leadership positions.

Influence & Affluence
of a Christian Worldview

Unique to the theme of "integration of Christian worldview" was the way in which it appeared to be woven. When the participants spoke about spiritual environment, it was incorporated into the context of other things that were part of the educational experience.

At times it seemed as if the connection between the integration of Christian worldview and the other themes were unconscious and natural, as if it was an expected and assumed part of everything else, but critically important. There were references to the importance of an integration of a biblical worldview in the academic context, to the example and interaction of faith with and from teachers, to the discussion and challenge of faith as well as spiritual lessons learned from conflicts and personal challenges, and to the role of spiritually driven activities. The context and environment of biblical integration provided examples of faith that they could emulate as teachers, as Christian role models who demonstrated commitment to following Christ and showing His love. Those same teachers, along with purposeful activities and curriculum, questioned and challenged their students' intellectual understanding of their beliefs, helping them to grow in the knowledge and application of their worldview. The provision of a safe community in which students could question, being challenged, and learning allowed them to develop coherence in their beliefs, resulting in their own commitment to a biblical worldview.

They identified this component as something that set their Christian school educational experience apart from other types of education. Participants in the study made specific connections between this theme and their own leadership development. In particular, they indicated that the establishment of their worldview was excellent. Ultimately, each of the interviews made some connection between their experiences and their leadership development. As they discussed and revealed the emergence of the themes, they would comment on how particular examples and events shaped the manner in which they now lead as an adult. They all indicated that their educational experience mattered, and it was an important component of their growth. As was previously stated, the common themes that emerged from the narratives were the influences and relationships the participants developed with teachers and pastors. Additionally, the importance of biblical integration throughout various learning experiences proved to be especially significant to the participants' leadership development; as it related to their Christian school experience.

The Importance of Education

The study focused on the attitudes and beliefs of administrators from around the country that show the call to renewal within the Christian school movement that will redefine the mission and vision. The survey was delivered through conversations with ten different administrators from various organizations. The survey was individually administered and contained only open-ended questions to allow participants to answer freely. The leaders chosen for this study were selected because of their distinguished service to the cause of Christian education, and/or their current involvement in the day to day operations of a Christian school. Several factors were taken into consideration when choosing participants for this study.

Regional location was one factor for the choice as well as longevity of commitment to the Christian education.

They also supported the applicability of Leadership Emergence Theory as a model for evaluating leadership development that occurs in the educational process, and for identifying patterns and principles to benefit and/or enhance the effectiveness of Christian education in its purpose of leadership development.

Several studies have addressed the issue of how life experiences influence the development of leadership (Hannah, 2006; White, 1998; Williams, 1996).

According to Leman and Pentak (2004), "each person you meet is a product of their life experiences. Often the key to understanding an individual . . . is to learn something about the person's various experiences".

A number of studies specifically identify the effect of educational experiences (or lack thereof) on the development of leadership, both in classroom experiences and in co-curricular experiences (Altman, 2006; Bloomer, 1999; Escobedo, 1998; Glass, 2012; O'Hearn & Blumer, 2008; Their, 1980; Waage, Paisley, & Gookin 2012; White, 1998).

The concept of Leadership Development Theory argues that leadership, particularly Christian leadership, develops over the lifetime of an individual as a result of experiences and is explained by the use of three variables (processing —developmental effect of critical spiritual incidents, time—the timeline along which development is measured, and response—reaction to spiritual processing) as they occur within a timeline of phases.

The stories of the participants indicated that their Christian school education influenced their leadership formation in a way that is consistent with the Leadership Emergence Theory model by revealing valid patterns, processes, and principles that were part of their experience. The conclusion is that this particular life experience, Christian education, can play an important role in the leadership development process ascribed to Leadership Emergence Theory. The results of this study, then, supported the applicability of Leadership Emergence Theory as a model for evaluating leadership development that occurs in the educational process and for identifying patterns and principles to benefit and/or enhance the effectiveness of Christian education in its purpose of development of leadership.

There are various studies on leadership that make a connection, both indirectly and directly, to shaping the influence of educational experiences. But while Leadership Emergence Theory has been fairly extensively analyzed and applied to leadership development, it has not been specifically applied to the realm of Christian education. Therefore, there would be value in more study on the relationship of Christian education to leadership development, because little research has been published regarding this connection. In today's relativistic world, many claim that, "it doesn't matter what you believe it's just important to believe something." No matter what the world would have one believe, sound doctrine is important. What one believes is critically important.

In the Book of Acts, the Bereans received the word with all

readiness, and searched the Scriptures daily to find out whether these things were so (Acts 17:11).

It is unfortunate that many Christians do not have a biblical worldview. Although, whether they know it or not, they have some sort of worldview.

A recent Barna survey reported that only 4% of American Christians had a biblical worldview. Because most Classical Christian schools teach and embrace solid, orthodox theology, their students will be much more likely to develop a biblical worldview.

A worldview is the way one looks at everything about them. It is the way that one interacts with the culture and, perhaps more importantly, the manner in which the culture affects the person.

The worldview of a person is vital because it affects the manner in which they think, speak, and behave in the world. At the risk of sounding overly Pavlovian, an individual's worldview is their "programming." A computer cannot do what it is not programmed to do. Likewise, a person will respond to an event or a statement by using what he or she has been taught at school, at home, at church, and in society in general. The biblical mandate for Christian education extends beyond the Christian school movement but also fuels the specific mission of Christian schools.

The Christian Philosophy of Education

What is a Christian philosophy of education?

Although the term Christian education does not occur in the Bible, the Bible speaks of the moral and spiritual instruction of believers in general and of children in particular. It places a high value upon knowledge, both of God and of His works. It describes the moral and spiritual fruits of this knowledge and defines its ultimate purpose.

The present Christian school movement can be understood only as a part-- certainly in these times a very significant and necessary part of the total endeavor of Christian education.

The Need for Christian Teachers

Biblical theological minds on education will cause us to think about teachers and teaching itself in ways that are both contrary and renewing to mainstream cultural conceptions. My preferred description of teachers and teaching for some time now has been:

Teachers are those who offer their lives to their students as worthy of imitation. To teach is to offer one's life to one's students as worthy of imitation.

I believe it was Augustine who asserted that if a person was a teacher then he or she was not evil; and if he or she was evil, then that person was not a teacher.

Understood in the light of biblical theology, it is a whole-of- life offering of oneself to one's students as worthy of imitation. In teaching there is, or ought to be, a vulnerability, an authentic vulnerability, appropriate to the age and maturity of students, that invites imitation. To think theologically about the task of teaching is to acknowledge that our task is primarily incarnational, inspirational and formational. These must be the grounds from which knowledge and skills are imparted. Expertise and brilliance must emanate from lives of virtue and character. And our formative goals will always occur in the context of educative influences that are de-formational for our students. What is it that is deforming or malforming our students in the 21st century cultures of which they are part? We need to be able to answer that question clearly if we hope to teach.

In this research, we offer an historical look at the importance of Christianity putting aside matters of theology or faith.

Impact on the Value of Human Life

Compassion and Mercy
Marriage and Family
Education
Government of the People
Science
Free Enterprise and the Work Ethic
Art, Music, Literature
Contrary Evidence

Summary

Christmas, of course, is to honor the birth of a humble Servant leader from the ancient world. Emperors and governors have come and gone, but it is this man, Jesus, whose birth we still celebrate over 2000 years later. We hope everyone can enjoy this account in the delightful spirit of Christmas. Even most non-Christians at least respect Jesus as a great moral teacher. In addition, few would argue that this one man has had more impact on the world than any person in history.

"Christianity is responsible for the way our society is organized and for the way we currently live. So extensive is the Christian contribution to our laws, our economics, our politics, our arts, our calendar, our holidays, and our moral and cultural priorities that historian J. M. Robers writes in The Triumph of the West, 'We could none of us today be what we are if a handful of Jews nearly two thousand years ago had not believed that they had known a great teacher, seen him crucified, dead, and buried, and then rise again.'

The Purpose of Christian Education:

Christian Education"—what does this term mean for the local church? Many local churches have a program for "Christian Education" (hereafter referred to as CE), yet there is not much standardization for the meaning or the purpose of such a program.

Christian Education programs include the traditional "Sunday School," but also include other planned programs of teaching, such as home Bible study groups, children's and youth ministries, and other teaching situations.

However, many churches have nothing in written form that promotes or organizes their CE program.

"Christian" is first used in Acts 11:26, where Barnabas goes to new believers in Antioch. Their attention to the teachings of Paul and Barnabas from the Word of God, apparently coupled with their steadfastness and obedience, gives rise to their being called "Christians." "Education" has a wide variety of definitions.

For the purpose of this project, it means to be taught from the Scriptures according to the command of Matthew 28:20. "Christian Education" must mean, as a result, teaching that imparts knowledge of God through the Scriptures and leads the student to living as Christ did, in obedience to God.

To put it another way, the goal of CE is to make mature Christians.

This is the task given to the local church by Jesus Christ. Christians are the people who are always talking about Christos, the Christ people . . . the adherents of Jesus Christ.

It seems clear that from Acts 11:26, the disciples were called Christians as a direct result of being taught, according to the command of Christ in Matthew 28:19, 20. A Handbook on the Acts of the Apostles says that the Christians were called by that name because they were adherents of Jesus Christ, not merely intellectual consumers.

Churches utilize a wide variety of approaches to Christian Education programs. Some follow curriculum developed by a denomination, some developed by a private company, and some churches write their own. The challenge is to develop a written, organized program that can be utilized by present and future leaders, with stated goals, which will provide teacher training.

However, there are many churches in which CE is a program that is conducted because "it has always been that way" and no one will challenge its operation or effectiveness. This does not result in making people "Christian," but only in creating consumers of religious knowledge. There exists a glaring need for training of teachers, evaluation and accountability.

Theological Basis

Scripture must be the source of the basis for an effective Christian Education. Kenneth O. Gangel says that there are two New Testament passages that provide the basis: Matthew 28:18-20 and Ephesians 4:11-16.

There is currently a lack of solid theological training for the local church member. Instead, an appeal to people's self-interest has spawned "the renewal movement," with teaching that emphasizes self-help and topics of interest, but provides little if any theological or doctrinal teaching. Findley Edge, a professor of the Southern Baptist Seminary, said that the "renewal movement emphasizes the external man to the exclusion of sound theology."

The Christian Commission

Go therefore —this phrase is filled with meaning as the basis for CE. Often it is said that this phrase refers to "as you are going" in the sense of being a disciple maker as one walks in his daily life. However, the meaning actually refers to a specific point of departure, or a specific decision to go and make disciples.

A Greek-English Lexicon of the New Testament and other Early Christian Literature says that this word, poreuomai, means a destination specified, to go, proceed, or travel.

The New International Dictionary of New Testament Theology says that this word means to go in a specific direction with a specific intention.

The work goes on to say that in the LXX, Judges 13:11 indicates following someone; and 1 Kings 14:8, obedience.

Then Genesis 22:2 and 2 Samuel 7:5 both indicate that God sends a man out on a particular path.

All of this clearly shows that the making of disciples is obedience to a specific command of God, and with the specific intention of the one obeying to make disciples.

Therefore, it cannot mean "as you go," as if making disciples was something one does as a sidelight of his walk with Christ.

Teach all nations"—This is an imperative verb, mathateuo, meaning to "teach, make disciples."

This is the primary command upon which the two commands to baptize and teach are built.

It is implied here one is becoming a disciple as well as going and training others to become disciples.

A true disciple will have a desire to reproduce others as disciples and will do whatever is necessary to accomplish this task.

Further, it is unnatural to beg a disciple to follow the Lord Jesus Christ and to obey this command.

The phrase "all nations" clearly indicates that everyone is included in the command. "Baptizing them in the name of the Father, Son, and Holy Spirit"—Rather than going into a lengthy discussion about the wording used in the act of baptizing, two major aspects need mention.

First, it is water baptism, as shown by Jesus' example (Matthew 3:13-16). Second, it is the beginning of formal fellowship within a local church, as indicated in Acts 2:41-47. Therefore, baptism is obedience to Christ's command and is part of becoming a disciple.

"Teaching them to observe everything I have commanded you"— This is the continuing work of all disciples: not only to learn (as the renewal movement stresses), but to train others.

The Foundations
of Christian Leadership

This project examines the role of calling (doing what God wants you to), competence (being good at what you do), confidence (knowing what you can accomplish in the context), and character ("good" traits) with the purpose of showing that character, while important, is the fourth in the sequence of the four.

The project draws from both Old Testament and New Testament examples of success based on each of the four Cs. The premise of the paper is that with each successful level of the four Cs, greater success happens.

An organization's leadership development program may be informed by this paper in that developing leaders should first be filtered/selected by their sense of calling, followed then by education and training to increase their competence.

Then, developing leaders can receive counseling and education to increase their confidence and finally, developing leaders can be coached, measured, critiqued, and developed in character traits.

A panel discussion at International School of Theology in 2008 during a doctoral program attempted to answer the question "What is Christian Leadership," and while concepts of qualities, characteristics, capabilities, and behaviors were addressed, the question seemed to be unanswered at the end.

As a participant of this panel, I was left with a gnawing uneasiness about what constituted a Christian or "Bible-based" leader.

It was during a 10-hour automobile drive with my spouse that the answer began to emerge.

My spouse stated her observation that some character-flawed old-testament leaders seemed to be blessed by God and that didn't seem to fit the general notion that "good" leaders are high-character leaders.

It was from this point that I began the search to understand what a Christian leader is and found four key elements in sequence – Calling, or doing the will of God, Competence, or doing what you do well, Confidence, or knowing what you can do by yourself and what you can do with God's help, and Character, or living a life according to Old Testament and New Testament character values.

This project presents these four concepts, along with a review of the literature on "what is a Christian Leader."

Calling

It seems appropriate to begin with Jesus' words. John 5:30 records Jesus' statement "I can do nothing on My own initiative. As I hear, I judge; and My judgment is just, because I do not seek My own will, but the will of Him who sent Me." What is translated as "will" in the last sentence is qelema (Thelema) that implies what God desires or commands.

The same word occurs eight times in the Gospel of John.

Competence

In contrast, anecdotal evidence from entrepreneurs who also went into business because of a call from God, but who had an education in business indicated that they were successful. In comparing the two groups, the anecdotal evidence shows that doing what you do well (competence) leads to a higher level of performance.

From the Old Testament beginning in Genesis and moving through the books, the following verses seem to support a need for competence. In Genesis 47:6 we find a call for capable men.

The land of Egypt is at your disposal; settle your father and your brothers in the best of the land, let them live in the land of Goshen; and if you know any capable men among them, then put them in charge of my livestock.

Continuing on in Exodus 31: 1-5 we find God advising Moses that He selected capable (competent) men.

Then the Lord said to Moses, "See, I have chosen Bezalel son of Uri, the son of Hur, of the tribe of Judah, and I have filled him with the Spirit of God, with skill, ability and knowledge in all kinds of crafts - to make artistic designs for work in gold, silver and bronze, to cut and set stones, to work in wood, and to engage in all kinds of craftsmanship".

In addition, in Exodus 35:25 we see that "skilled" workers were selected to make elements for the tent of meeting. It is interesting to note that preceding this mention of "skilled" the text in Exodus 35:21 says that these people's hearts were stirred by God (called).

Exodus 35:21: Everyone whose heart stirred him and everyone whose spirit moved him came and brought the LORD'S contribution for the work of the tent of meeting and for all its service and for the holy garments.

Exodus 35:25: All the skilled women spun with their hands, and brought they had spun, {in} blue and purple {and} scarlet {material} and {in} fine linen.

We see in 1Kings 7:14 that it was first wisdom and understanding (competence in thought) and then skill (competence in craft) that preceded Hiram's employment by King Solomon.

He was a widow's son from the tribe of Naphtali, and his father was a man of Tyre, a worker in bronze; and he was filled with wisdom and understanding and skill for doing any work in bronze. So he came to King Solomon and performed all his work.

From 1 Chronicles 26:30 and 32 we see reference to the need to have capable people.

1 Chronicles 26:30: As for the Hebronites, Hashabiah and his relatives, 1,700 capable men, had charge of the affairs of Israel west of the Jordan, for all the work of the LORD and the service of the king.

1 Chronicles 26:32: and his relatives, capable men, {were} 2,700 in number, heads of fathers' {households}. And King David made them overseers of the Reubenites, the Gadites and the half-tribe of the Manassites concerning all the affairs of God and of the king.

Continuing with evidence from the Old Testament, we find in 2 Chronicles 2:7 and 2:13-14 that "skilled" people are needed and desired.

2 Chronicles 2:7: Now send me a skilled man to work in gold, silver, brass and iron, and in purple, crimson and violet {fabrics}, and who knows how to make engravings, to {work} with the skilled men whom I have in Judah and Jerusalem, whom David my father provided.

2 Chronicles 2:13 – 14 Now I am sending Huram-abi, a skilled man, endowed with understanding, the son of a Danite woman and a Tyrian father, who knows how to work in gold, silver, bronze, iron, stone and wood, {and} in purple, violet, linen and crimson fabrics, and {who knows how} to make all kinds of engravings and to execute any design which may be assigned to him, {to work} with your skilled men and with those of my lord David your father.

From Proverbs 22:29 we find a compelling argument for competence.

Do you see a man skilled in his work? He will stand before kings; He will not stand before obscure men.

In Jeremiah 10:9 we find yet another reference to competence in the terms of "craftsman" and "skilled men."

Beaten silver is brought from Tarshish, and gold from Uphaz, The work of a craftsman and of the hands of a goldsmith; Violet and purple are their clothing; They are all the work of skilled men.

From Ezra 7:1-10 we see that the hand of God was upon him (a calling) that preceded Ezra's action of studying and practicing the law of the Lord even though the text shows that he was already skilled in the law of Moses.

Now after these things, in the reign of Artaxerxes king of Persia, {there went up} Ezra son of Seraiah, son of Azariah, son of Hilkiah, son of Shallum, son of Zadok, son of Ahitub, son of Amariah, son of Azariah, son of Meraioth, son of Zerahiah, son of Uzzi, son of Bukki, son of Abishua, son of Phinehas, son of Eleazar, son of Aaron the chief priest.

This Ezra went up from Babylon, and he was a scribe skilled in the law of Moses, which the LORD God of Israel had given; and the king granted him all he requested because the hand of the LORD his God {was} upon him. Some of the sons of Israel and some of the priests, the Levites, the singers, the gatekeepers and the temple servants went up to Jerusalem in the seventh year of King Artaxerxes. He came to Jerusalem in the fifth month, which was in the seventh year of the king. For on the first of the first month he began to go up from Babylon; and on the first of the fifth month he came to Jerusalem, because the good hand of his God {was} upon him. For Ezra had set his heart to study the law of the LORD and to practice {it}, and to teach {His} statutes and ordinances in Israel. (NAS)

Competence does not always align with doing what is good but can, as we see in Ezekiel 21:31 and in Daniel 8:23, apply to doing what is not considered good but still doing it well. Exekiel 21:31: I will pour out My indignation on you; I will blow on you with the fire of My wrath, and I will give you into the hand of brutal men, skilled in destruction.

Daniel 8:23: In the latter period of their rule, When the transgressors have run {their course}, A king will arise, insolent and skilled in intrigue.

Colossians 3:34-24 gives a sense of the need to do what we do well, from which we can derive a need for competence. Whatever you do, work at it with all your heart, as working for the Lord, not for men, since you know that you will receive an inheritance from the Lord as a reward. It is the Lord Christ you are serving.

In summary, the verses presented above all refer to the need to be good at what we do. While from the prior section on calling it is clear that calling without competence can still lead to success – calling with confidence should lead to greater success.

Confidence

Even with calling and competence, success may not occur to the level that it could if the leader lacks confidence. The notion of confidence is similar to the concept of self-efficacy (Bandura, 1994) in that people perceive their ability to do or not do something.

The focus here is on self-perception, rather than reality. While it is possible and probable that perception matches reality, it is perception that drives this concept. Successes and failures contribute to a perception of self-efficacy, although when faced with unfamiliar situations, experience is replaced with self-beliefs of the individual.

We can see an account of this in the account of Elijah's confrontation with Baal's priests and then Elijah's subsequent confrontation with Jezebel. In 1 Kings 18 we find Elijah engaging the Priests and challenging them to a contest in which the priests of Baal would call upon their god to bring fire down and light the sacrificial fire.

After the priests of Baal failed, Elijah took his turn and increased the difficulty by soaking the wood and the offering with water. Filled with confidence, Elijah prayed and fire came from Heaven and consumed not only the wood and the offering but the entire altar.

1Kings 18:38: Then the fire of the LORD fell and consumed the burnt offering and the wood and the stones and the dust, and licked up the water that was in the trench.

Following this success, the account in 1 Kings 18 says that Elijah then killed the 450 prophets of Baal.

This is a demonstration of calling, competence, and confidence. However, following Elijah's success, which should have increased his perception of his self-efficacy, Elijah learns that Jezebel is angry with him and seeks his demise as accounted in 1Kings 19:1-4. In this account, we see a lack of confidence from Elijah in that while he faced and killed 450 prophets, he now is ready to give up when faced with one woman.

Now Ahab told Jezebel all that Elijah had done, and how he had killed all the prophets with the sword. Then Jezebel sent a messenger to Elijah, saying, "So may the gods do to me and even more, if I do not make your life as the life of one of them by tomorrow about this time." And he was afraid and arose and ran for his life and came to Beersheba, which belongs to Judah, and left his servant there. But he himself went a day's journey into the wilderness and came and sat down under a juniper tree; and he requested for himself that he might die, and said, "It is enough; now, O LORD, take my life, for I am not better than my fathers.

From Matthew 14:28-31 we see an example of both confidence and a lack of confidence in the account of Peter asking Jesus to let Peter walk on the water.

Peter said to Him, "Lord, if it is You, command me to come to You on the water." And He said, "Come!" And Peter got out of the boat, and walked on the water and came toward Jesus.

But seeing the wind, he became frightened, and beginning to sink, he cried out, "Lord, save me!" Immediately Jesus stretched out His hand and took hold of him, and said to him, "You of little faith, why did you doubt?"

Character

In addition to the prior elements of calling, competence, and confidence, character is a key element of Christian (biblical) leadership as evidenced in the passages of Psalms 1 and 15; The Beatitudes, Philemon, 1 Peter, and 2 Peter 1:5-1. Character, although in the fourth position of the four Cs, has a significant amount of material since it seems that there is a general sense that character is the most important. This is not borne out though when one looks at the character of Moses when he killed the Egyptian Exodus 2:14: But he said, "Who made you a prince or a judge over us? Are you intending to kill me as you killed the Egyptian?" Then Moses was afraid and said, "Surely the matter has become known."

Abraham when he presented his wife as his sister to the King Genesis 20:2: Abraham said of Sarah his wife, "She is my sister." So King Abimelech sent and took Sarah.

When David committed adultery, although there was a severe penalty later in this life, he continued to be successful for quite some time. 2 Samuel 11: 3-4: So David sent and inquired about the woman. And one said, "Is this not Bathsheba, the daughter of Eliam, the wife of Uriah the Hittite?" David sent messengers and took her, and when she came to him, he lay with her; and when she had purified herself from her uncleanness, she returned to her house.

The historical accounts of Ahab indicates that he was successful in his 11 to 19-year reign. Ahab, the son of Omri, did evil in the sight of the LORD more than all who were before him. Thus, from the verses above, we can see that character is not the determinant for success. While Ahab did not show calling or character, he did show competence and confidence, the other references above showed both calling, competence, and confidence in what they did. The sections that follow show both character and behavior in which the behavior is the outgrowth of the character.

Psalms 1 provides us with a view of the righteous leader who, through his/her beliefs, demonstrates characteristics in line with biblical principles.

The passage below shows that a "blessed" leader does not interact with the wicked nor participate with evil people.

Psalms 1:1-6: How blessed is the man who does not walk in the counsel of the wicked, nor stand in the path of sinners, nor sit in the seat of scoffers! But his delight is in the law of the LORD, and on His law he meditates day and night.

In conclusion, I think Christian education is key in this era. There is a need for Christian leaders in the schools, community and law enforcement.

I would like to thank you for this opportunity share through research and conviction.

I pray that the research will really bless you, all Christians should support Christian education.

Should we all study? Yes, everyone should study the Bible!

Why Study the Bible?

Introduction

The most obvious reason to study the Bible is because God said it.

2 Tim 2:15 During Paul's second missionary journey, when he and Silas arrived at Berea in Macedonia, Acts 17:11 says of the Bereans, "These were more noble than those in Thessalonica, in that they received the word with all readiness of mind, and searched the scriptures daily, whether those things were so." Note that the Bereans searched the scriptures, not one day a week, but daily, and with minds that were open to God's truths.

The Bible is no ordinary book. The words within its pages are like medicine to your soul. It has the power to change your life because there is life in the Word! (Hebrews 4:12.) And when you discover the power and truth of God's Word, you will begin to see changes in your life that only this truth can bring. You will even learn how to recognize what the enemy tries to bring against you.

Proverbs 4:20-22 says, "My son attend to my words...for they are life to those who find them..." The word "attend" means to pay attention to, give some time to something. To attend to the Word of God is a lot more than just reading; it's meditating on it. We need to get into agreement with what God wants us to do because, as the writer of Proverbs says, these words are life! When you need an encouraging word, or you're in a negative environment, it's good to know that you can find life (plus healing and health) in God's Word.

What Do I Study?

There's really no wrong place to start. You can study anything that's going to help you. If you're dealing with anger or fear, flip to the back of your Bible's concordance and locate those words to see which scriptures talk about those subjects.

Recommended Study Tools

Thompson Chain Reference Bible – cross references about different topics throughout the Bible

Webster's Dictionary Strong's Exhaustive Concordance – listing of scriptures organized by category/ topic

Vine's Expository Dictionary – Greek and Hebrew definitions.

Here are four steps you can take to begin digging into God's Word:

Four Effective Steps to Studying the Bible

1. Purposely set aside time. I personally study in the mornings, but if that doesn't work for you, find a time that does…even if it's not every day. Whatever you can do, that's what you need to do. Just start somewhere and you'll see the fruit that this time brings to your life!
2. Make preparation for your Bible study. Have a place that you enjoy being—a room in your home where you can be alone. Somewhere you are comfortable and like to be.
3. Have all your materials available. You'll want of course your Bible, but also get a good Bible dictionary, concordance, a pen and paper. So that, you don't have to stop every few minutes to reference something or write something down.
4. Prepare your heart. Talk to God about things you may need to confess, and enter your study time peacefully and without anything that may block you from receiving illumination during your study.

Make the time in your life to study because there is power in it to change your life and become the person God wants you to be. Once you do, you'll experience the peace and joy to enjoy every day of your life!

Why should we study the Bible?

To some of you the reasons may be obvious. But just as children cannot grow to be strong without meat, new Christians must partake of the meat of the Word of God in order to mature as believers (1 Corinthians 3:1-2 and Hebrews 5:12-14).

Even mature believers who have studied the scriptures for years can still uncover many more precious truths in God's Word.

When instructing Timothy in the ministry, Apostle Paul wrote in 2 Timothy 2:15, "Study to shew thyself approved of God, a workman that needeth not to be ashamed, rightly dividing the word of truth."

This call to Bible study echos an earlier point that Paul had made in 1 Timothy 5:17, "Let the elders that rule well be counted worthy of double honour, especially they who labour in the word and doctrine." How can one eat with their mouth closed?

In in Ephesians 6:11, Paul instructs the believer to, "Put on the whole armour of God, that ye may be able to stand against the wiles of the devil." A few verses later in Ephesians 6:17 he explains that part of that armour of God is "... the sword of the Spirit, which is the word of God .... In Matthew 4:4, Jesus Christ says, "... Man shall not live by bread alone, but by every word that proceedeth out of the mouth of God."

Many churches use quarterly booklets that cover ten or so Bible verses each week, and boast that the quarterlies cover the entire Bible in seven years. But at that rate, only about ten percent of the Bible can be covered. This falls far short of being "every word that proceedeth out of the mouth of god."

Isaiah 34:16 says, "Seek ye out the book of the LORD, and read: no one of these shall fail ...." With this verse occuring in the midst of a passage filled with prophecies, it not only calls for study of the Bible in general, but also more specifically, it calls for the study of Bible prophecy. Even among those Christians who do study the Bible, there are many who make an effort to steer clear of studying Bible prophecy, and there are many churches that make a point of avoiding the study of Bible prophecy.

The Old Testament prophetic books from Isaiah to Malachi alone are more than twenty percent of the Bible. The book of Revelation and substantial portions of almost every other book of the Bible are also prophetic. Prophecy is found in the teachings of Jesus Christ during His earthly ministry, and in the inspired letters written by Paul, Peter, and Jude. Genesis, the books of the law, the books of Samuel, the books of Kings, and Psalms also contain large amounts of prophecy.

Peter wrote in 2 Peter 1:19, "We have also a more sure word of prophecy: whereunto ye do well that ye take heed, as unto a light that shineth in a dark place ...." This statement is even more remarkable considering the context. Peter had just been describing great things which he had witnessed with his own eyes and ears. In the preceding verses, Peter had described what he, John, and James witnessed when Jesus Christ was transfigured before them on the mountain in Matthew 17:2-5. He says in 2 Peter 1:16-18, "For we have not followed cunningly devised fables, when we made known unto you the power and coming of our Lord Jesus Christ, but were eyewitnesses of his majesty. For he received from God the Father honour and glory, when there came such a voice to him from the excellent glory, This is my beloved Son, in whom I am well pleased. And this voice which came from heaven we heard, when we were with him in the holy mount."

We cannot imagine the awesome power and majesty of this event. Yet Peter follows this by saying that the word of prophecy is even "more sure" than that, as "a light that shineth in a dark place".

Revelation 1:3 says that those who read or hear prophetic words of the book of Revelation will be blessed. "Blessed is he that readeth, and they that hear the words of this prophecy, and keep those things which are written therein: for the time is at hand."

One final reason that we should study Bible prophecy is that when we study the Word of God, we need to understand the context of the passage that we are reading.

To avoid taking scriptures out of the appropriate context, we need to see the prophetic framework of God's whole plan for the ages. Prophecy provides both the background (history) and the foreground (future) information that is essential to understanding each passage from the Word of God in its intended context.

Christian education is not simply education for education's sake, nor is it merely driven by pragmatic necessities; rather, it is a ministry of the church. Education that seeks simply to impart knowledge or raise levels of cognition or awareness falls short of education as a calling to pastoral service within the community of faith. Christian educators must never forget that we are first pastors and then educators and that education serves the pastoral function of nurturing faith within the community of the church.

Project Interviews

Dr. Cordelia Moffett - Dr. Moffett is a Christian who loves God and people. She also is a retired educator of the Phenix City, AL School System. Dr. Moffett has served the community well for 39 years, as a teacher, principle and Asst. Superintendent. She is a devoted disciple of the Nichols Chapel A.M.E. Church located in Phenix City, AL. God has tremendously used this woman of God both in Christian and secular work.

Elizabeth Morris- Ms. Morris is a retired Educator of the Russell County, AL School System for 35 years. She is a disciple of the Mt. Olive Baptist Church, where she currently serves as Administrative assistant for more than 20 years. She certainly displays the true attributes of a Christian. She is a very hard worker in the church and community.

Annie Lindsey- Mrs. Lindsey is truly a servant of God, a motivator, encourager and Christian leader. Mrs. Lindsey is very concerned with the world's view of Christian education. She feels that teaching is a calling from God. She possesses a demanding voice that calls for the attention of young men and young ladies. She is an educator for the Phenix City, AL Schools. We are certainly grateful for her servitude for 35 years.

Xavier Maddox- Pastor Maddox is the pastor of the 24th street Baptist Church of Columbus, GA. What a voice crying in the wilderness. He is a professor of homiletics, and Pastoral Theology. He has certainly lead this area faithfully. He is a family man. He has 32 years in pastoral ministry.

Sheriff Heath Taylor- Heath Taylor is the sheriff of Russell county.

He is a Southern Baptist and is a disciple of the Golden Acres Baptist Church of Phenix City, Alabama.

Patricia Alexander- Patricia Alexander has served the Phenix City, AL and Muscogee County, GA School Systems for over 30 years. She is a member of the Mt. Olive Baptist Church, where she faithfully serves as the historian and church announcer along with a lot of other activities.

Dr. Charles Kelly- Dr. Kelly is the Moderator of the East Alabama Missionary Baptist Progressive District Association of Phenix City, AL and Germany. He served this country well in the Vietnam War and continues to serve the Captain of his Salvation.

Pastor Terrance Brown - Pastor Brown is the servant leader of the Worship Center in Baltimore, Maryland. He is a computer scientist who utilizes his gifts to help mold the minds of young men in community. Additionally, has a very powerful evangelistic ministry in which feeds the community where he dwells.

Dr. Grey Edwards- Dr. Edwards is the educational director of the Ft. Bennington Military Campus. He is a Christian gentleman who loves God and loves people. He is a Sunday school teacher and has been in the area of education for 45 years or more.

Robert Bradley- Robert Bradley is a Christian who serves as the chairman of Deacons at the Bethel Baptist Church in Borger, TX. He is a profound teacher of the Bible and he is president of the School system.

References

Altman, R. (2006). Issues and observations: Leadership lessons from a scrap- book. Leadership in Action, 26(3), 21-22.

Bandura, A. (1969). Principles of behavior modification. New York, NY: Holt, Rinehart, & Winston.

Bandura, A. (1986). Social foundations of thought and action: A social cognitive theory. Englewood Cliffs, NJ: Prentice-Hall.

Bandura, A. (2003). On the psychosocial impact and mechanisms of spiritual modeling. International Journal for the Psychology of Religion, 13(3), 167.

Barna Group. (2013). Christians on leadership, calling, and career. Ventura, CA: Author.

Bloomer, T. A. (1999). Formative educational experiences of leaders as factors influencing innovation in organizations (Unpublished doctoral dissertation). Trinity Evangelical Divinity School, Deerfield, Illinois.

Burns, J. M. (1978). Leadership. New York, NY: Harper & Row.

Hoekstra, L. (2012). Middle school teachers' perspectives regarding the under- standing, knowledge, and practice of integrating faith and learning in Christian schools of the reformed tradition: A phenomenological study (Unpublished doctoral dissertation). Azusa Pacific University, Azusa, California.

Horn, Jr., T. W. (2005). Developmental processes critical to the formation of servant leaders in China (Unpublished doctoral dissertation). Andrews University, Berrien Springs, Michigan.

Kim, Y., & Sax, L. (2009). Student-faculty interaction in research universities: Differences by student gender, race, social class, and first-generation status. Research in Higher Education, 50(5), 437-459.

Kimbrough, L. C. (2007). Perceptions of leader ethical behavior and its relation- ship to organizational effectiveness: An exploratory study (Unpublished doctoral dissertation). Capella University, Minneapolis, Minnesota.

King, K. A., Vidourek, R. A., Davis, B., & McClellan W. (2002). Increasing self- esteem and school connectedness through a multidimensional mentoring program. Journal of School Health, 72(7), 294.

Kouzes, J. M., & Posner, B. Z. (2002). The leadership challenge. San Francisco, CA: Jossey-Bass.

Kouzes, J. M., & Posner, B. Z. (Eds.). (2004). Christian reflections on the leadership challenge. San Francisco, CA: Jossey-Bass.

Krispin, Jr., K. R. (2004). The relationship between youth ministry involvement and faith maturity in first-year students in a Christian college (Unpublished doctoral dissertation). Southern Baptist Theological Seminary, Louisville, Kentucky.

Leman, K., & Pentak, W. (2004). The way of the shepherd. Grand Rapids, MI: Zondervan.

Lund, J. W. (2007). Successful faculty mentoring relationships at evangelical Christian colleges. Christian Higher Education, 6(5), 371-390.

Martin, A. J., & Dowson, M. (2009). Interpersonal relationships, motivation, engagement, and achievement: Yields for theory, current issues, and educational practice. Review of Educational Research, 79(1), 327-365.

Martin, A. J., Marsh, H. W., McInerney, D. M., Green, J., & Dowson, M. (2007). Getting along with teachers and parents: The yields of good relationships for students' achievement motivation and self-esteem. Australian Journal of Guidance & Counselling, 17(2), 109-125.

Matchett, N. (2009). Cooperative learning, critical thinking, and character. Public Integrity, 12(1), 25-38

McMillan, J. H., & Schumacher, S. (2001). Research in education. New York, NY: Addison Wesley Longman.

Merriam, S. B. (1998). Qualitative research and case study applications in education. San Francisco, CA: Jossey-Bass.

Notes

Notes

Notes

Notes